P9-DBX-851

RAIN

BY HARRIET BRUNDLE

Weather
Explorers

Weather
Explorers

©2016
Book Life
King's Lynn
Norfolk
PE30 4LS

ISBN: 978-1-910512-71-5

All rights reserved
Printed in China
Written by:
Harriet Brundle
Edited by:
Amy Allatson
Designed by:
Drue Rintoul

A catalogue record for this book
is available from the British Library.

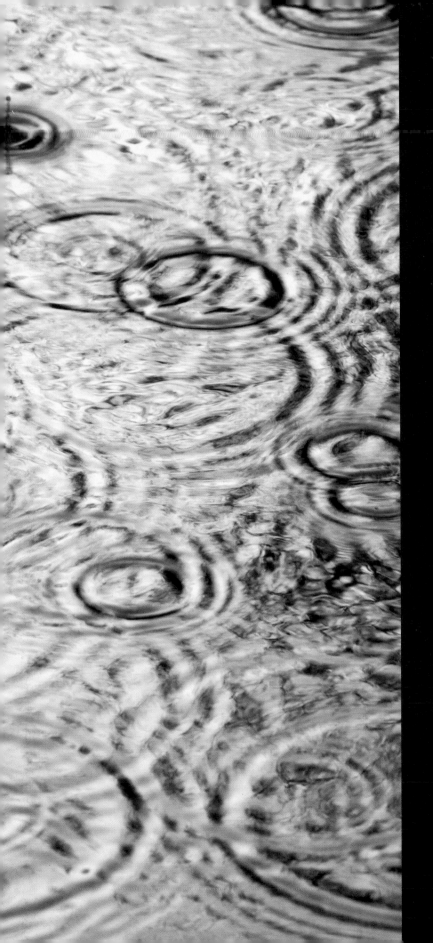

CONTENTS

Words in **bold** can be found in the glossary on page 24.

RAIN

When drops of water fall
from the sky, it is raining.

4

If the sun shines while it is raining, a rainbow appears!

HOW DOES RAIN HAPPEN?

RAINDROPS

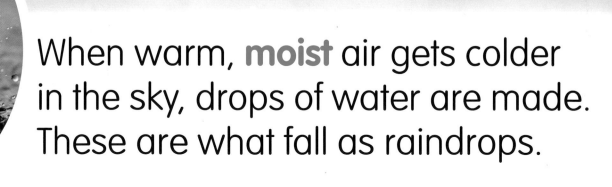

When warm, **moist** air gets colder in the sky, drops of water are made. These are what fall as raindrops.

The rain falls onto the ground. Some goes into the ground and some stays on the **surface**.

PUDDLE

THE WATER CYCLE

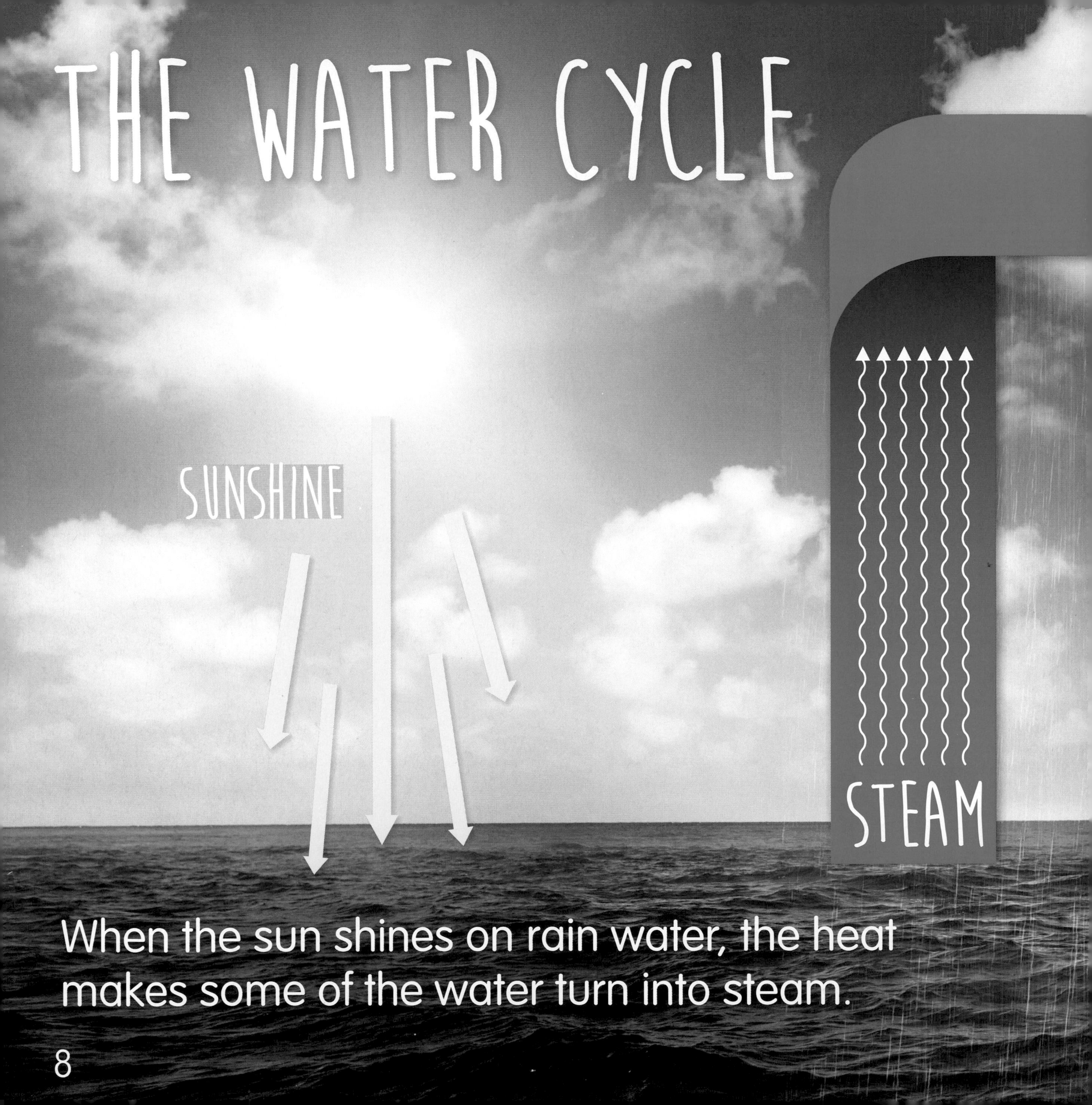

SUNSHINE

STEAM

When the sun shines on rain water, the heat makes some of the water turn into steam.

The steam goes up into the air. When it cools down, it falls as rain and the cycle starts again.

RAIN

RAIN AND THE SEASONS

There are four seasons in a year.

SPRING

SUMMER

WINTER

AUTUMN

Winter has the highest amount of rainfall. The winter months are December, January and February.

January						
Sun	Mon	Tue	Wed	Thu	Fri	Sat
	2	3	4	5	6	7
	9	10	11	12	13	14
	16	17	18	19	20	21
	23	24	25	26	27	28
	30	31				

February						
Sun	Mon	Tue	Wed	Thu	Fri	Sat
		1	2	3	4
5	6	7	8	9	10	11
12	13	14	15	16	17	18
19	20	21	22	23	24	25
	27	28	29			

March						
Sun	Mon	Tue	Wed	Thu	Fri	Sat
			1	2	3
4	5	6	7	8	9	10
11	12	13	14	15	16	17
18	19	20	21	22	23	24
25	26	27	28	29	30	31

April						
Sun	Mon	Tue	Wed	Thu	Fri	Sat
	2	3	4	5	6	7
	9	10	11	12	13	14
	16	17	18	19	20	21
	23	24	25	26	27	28
	30					

May						
Sun	Mon	Tue	Wed	Thu	Fri	Sat
	1	2	3	4	5
7	8	9	10	11	12
14	15	16	17	18	19
21	22	23	24	25	26
28	29	30	31		

June						
Sun	Mon	Tue	Wed	Thu	Fri	Sat
				1	2
3	4	5	6	7	8	9
10	11	12	13	14	15	16
17	18	19	20	21	22	23
24	25	26	27	28	29	30

July						
Sun	Mon	Tue	Wed	Thu	Fri	Sat
	2	3	4	5	6	7
	9	10	11	12	13	14
	16	17	18	19	20	21
	23	24	25	26	27	28
	30	31				

August						
Sun	Mon	Tue	Wed	Thu	Fri	Sat
		1	2	3	4
6	7	8	9	10	11
13	14	15	16	17	18
20	21	22	23	24	25
27	28	29	30	31	

September						
Sun	Mon	Tue	Wed	Thu	Fri	Sat
					1
3	4	5	6	7	8
10	11	12	13	14	15
17	18	19	20	21	22
24	25	26	27	28	29

October						
Sun	Mon	Tue	Wed	Thu	Fri	Sat
1	2	3	4	5	6
8	9	10	11	12	13
15	16	17	18	19	20
22	23	24	25	26	27
29	30	31			

November						
Sun	Mon	Tue	Wed	Thu	Fri	Sat
			1	2	3
5	6	7	8	9	10
12	13	14	15	16	17
19	20	21	22	23	24
26	27	28	29	30	

December						
Sun	Mon	Tue	Wed	Thu	Fri	Sat
					1
3	4	5	6	7	8
10	11	12	13	14	15
17	18	19	20	21	22
24	25	26	27	28	29
31						

There is often rain in the other seasons too.

We have the least rainfall in summertime. The summer is the warmest and driest season.

WHAT DO WE WEAR?

When it is raining we need to stay dry. We wear coats to protect us from the rain.

RAINCOAT

WELLINGTON BOOTS

To keep our feet dry, we wear Wellington boots.

PLANTS

Plants need water to grow bigger. When it rains, we don't need to give them any extra water.

Some plants live in places where there is hardly any rain.

CACTUS

CACTI KEEP WATER INSIDE THEIR STEMS FOR MANY MONTHS.

ANIMALS

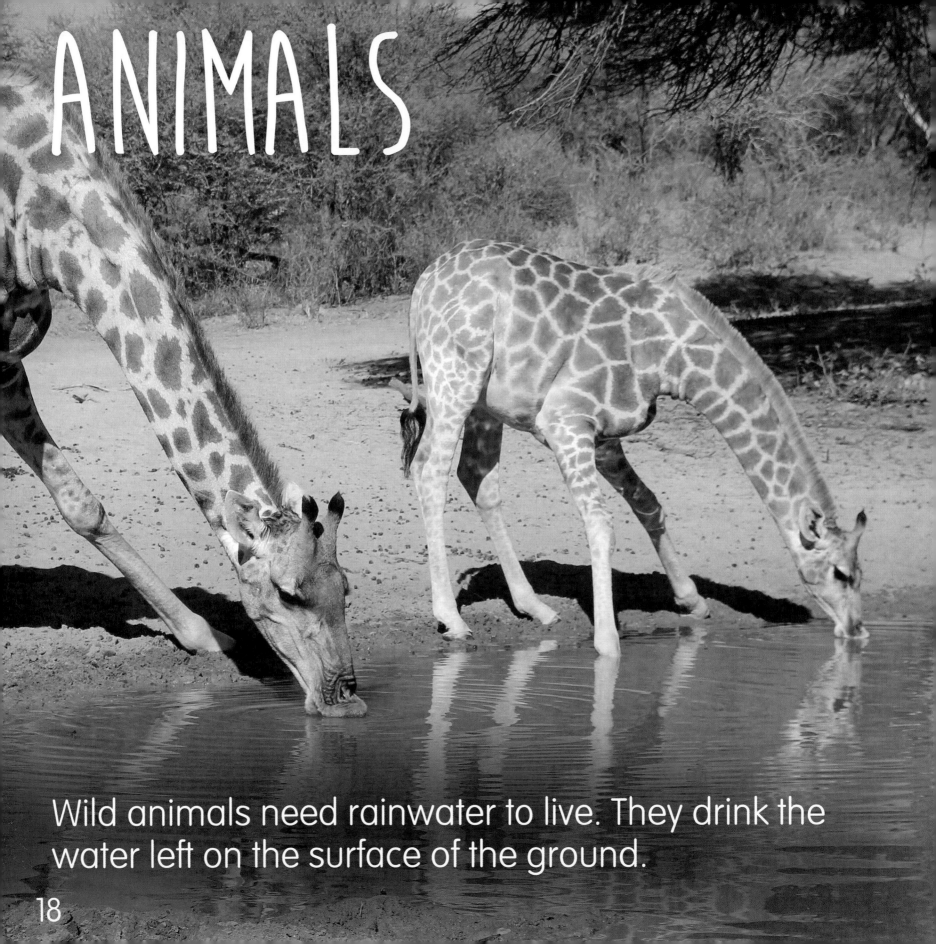

Wild animals need rainwater to live. They drink the water left on the surface of the ground.

Some animals don't like the rain.
They hide away so they don't get wet.

FLOODS

When there is too much rain, it can cause a flood.

SANDBAGS

The flood water can be dangerous.
We use **flood defences** to protect us.

DID YOU KNOW?

SNOWFLAKE

Water can also fall from the sky as snow. This happens when raindrops freeze!

22

Rain mostly happens as a drizzle or a shower. A shower is when the raindrops fall quickly and there are lots of them. When it drizzles, the rain is lighter and lasts longer.

GLOSSARY

Flood Defences: ways of protecting us from flood water.

Moist: slightly wet or damp.

Surface: the outside part of something.

Photocredits: Abbreviations: l-left, r-right, b-bottom, t-top, c-centre, m-middle.
All images are courtesy of Shutterstock.com.

Front Cover – mythja. 1 – Stockagogo, Craig Barhorst. 2-3 – Mr Twister. 4 – FamVeld. 5 – andreiuc88. 5insett – Serg64. 5insetb – peresanz. 6 – Kirill Smirnov. 6inset – Janis Smits. 7 – Dasha Petrenko. 8-9 – Iakov Kalinin. 10tl – Drew Rawcliffe. 10tr – Sunny studio. 10bl – Steve Horsley. 10br – balounm. 11 – JonesHon. 12 – Natalia Kirichenko. 12rt – fotohunter. 12rm – Monika Gniot. 12rb – Ase. 13 – Rohappy. 14 – A Jackson. 15 – Dasha Petrenko. 16 – igor.stevanovic. 17 – Anton Foltin. 18 – Stacey Ann Alberts. 19 – czechphotos. 20 – Paolo Bona. 21 – weerayut ranmai. 22 – Sunny Forest. 22inset – Jefunne. 23 – Patrick Foto. 24 – Grisha Bruev.

GUILDERLAND PUBLIC LIBRARY
2228 WESTERN AVENUE
GUILDERLAND, NY 12084
518-456-2400